GOD

Yes, I had put down writing, but it seems I cannot get away from the Michelle Jean Line of Books for some reason.

Yes, my ordination. Therefore, I cannot run from God. I cannot stop doing what God has and have asked me to do.

Body is so gone right now. Went to my dad's and cleaned his place as well as, got his paperwork done that he needed to get done.

Body needs warmth right now. My eldest son picked me up and I am so grateful. I could not do my dad's laundry because he said someone told him there were bugs – bed bugs in the laundry. I did not want to take the chance of doing his laundry downstairs. So, I am waiting until later to call my older brother to see if he can pick me up, take me to my dad's home so that I can take his laundry to an outside laundry mat to do his clothes.

This morning (May 10th, 2021), I dreamt Mikhail Prokhorov. I do not know what the hell is going on in Russia and you know what, I will not concern myself with Russia.

In the dream I was in his home and this Young Black Guy was in his home as well. The Young Black Guy picked up one of Prokhorov's gun, and he Prokhorov took up a bigger gun. You know what. Let me forget it because the guns were black and huge.

I truly do not know what people see in destructive things – death. Yes, Prokhorov took the gun from the Young Black Guy, and in the end, I was hugging and kissing Prokhorov.

So don't know if he's being targeted for death, theft, or whatever.

Truly not going to analyze that dream because something is truly not right with Russia. I truly hope African Lands, or any Black Land do not get involved with Russia gun wise, military wise, war wise, death wise, and more. *HELL IS NOT THE ANSWER FOR BLACK PEOPLE PERIOD. Death is truly not the answer to life.* Death is the answer to Death period.

No. To what I write and know about Hell, why would Young Black People continue to pick up the gun? Protect your damned life and soul come on now. *ENOUGH BLACK PEOPLE IS IN HELL ALREADY. DO NOT STRIVE TO GO TO HELL AND BURN COME ON NOW.*

Was this the way I wanted to start off this book?

"No"

This is the way I wanted to start off this book.

You know some family members are bitches.

No for real everyone. *SOME FAMILY MEMBERS ARE BITCHES.* All they think of is themself and though they say they care about you, F them because they care not for you. It's just words for them to get what they want out of you therefore, *F FAMILY.*

No, I loathe family that are red yie, greedy; plain out disgusting to the way they are greedy and manipulative.

I live by certain principles, but you have some family that live to cheat; *are all out worthless.*

Be fair and just in life come on now.

No, I am pissed to what my sister called me and told me about what my uncle said, and I told her no. Yes, I could hear the disappointment in her voice but, it's what it is when it comes to me. Life isn't about greed or taking what truly do not belong to you. Don't use people or family period. Think, and be fair come on now.

My sister and I did not talk for long. She said she would call me back, but she never did.

I truly love truth but it's not all that can be truthful, fair, just, as well as live by the truth of Them and God. Therefore, I truly stay away from family when I know certain things.

Well, I stay away from my family period. I am one away as some of us Jamaicans would say.

Every family have issues yes, but you do have some that *DEVOUR YOU; KILL YOU FI DEAD LEF.*

I MORE THAN CATEGORICALLY REFUSE TO FIGHT ANYONE FI DEAD LEF.

Respect yourself man come on now.

It is so disgusting to the way people fight for what truly do not belong to them.

It is so disgusting to the way people fight over *DEAD LEF.*

No, any of my children fight over what I leave, I give you my word in the *LIVING AND IN DEATH THAT EVERYONE OF THEM WOULD LOSE IT ALL.*

It is a disgusting and immoral person that would fight over *DEAD LEF;* what truly do not belong to them.

If a person truly thought of you in the living, they would have been fair and just to you in the living _so that when they die, you have absolutely nothing to worry about once they have passed on; died._ But, you have people that are truly not satisfied therefore, they go to every and any lengths to fight you down for what was given to you.

HOGS ARE THOSE WHO FIGHT FI DEAD LEF. And I will not take these words back. Therefore, humans fight for all that is wrong.

I truly have to thank Lovey for the way he made me.

What do not belong to me truly do not belong to me and I refuse to fight you down for what is yours.

My mother and grandmother instilled good values in me. So, no, my uncle need(s) to look into himself and see his own greed and worthlessness if he can. And, I truly do not care if he hates me for these words. Right is right and wrong is wrong come on now.

Michelle

I so have to have patience in life. It's May 11, 2021 and my dream world wow.

Was the Moon trying to contact me via my dream world?

Yes, but we did not connect.

Did I dream about the Georgian Bay, Muskoka Region?

Yes

Dreamt melting snow, kids, and white people. I was walking amongst homes and the river and or, lake was high with snow. There were no barriers for the homes. If the snow fully melted, the homes would flood. But with the Lake being so close to road level, I thought that was not good.

I so do not want to get into the dream fully because in the dream, the land was eroding, and there was this part where you could see the erosion and I was helping this white guy, and girl to fill the hole. There was also this black dog in the dream that began to lick the white guy. The dog had something attached to it that was long. I would say long tape worm but in the dream, it was not a tape worm.

Further, apparently it was not the first time the land in the Georgian Bay, Muskoka Region had eroded and had to be fixed.

You know what let me stop because LAND IS GOING TO START ERODING MORE AND MORE IN CANADA and I am going to leave it at that.

Further, I do not know if dogs are going to get infected and pass their infection on to their owners or if the Georgian Bay, Muskoka Region is going to be flooded soon. All I know is:

SOMETHING IS NOT RIGHT PEOPLE WISE AND ENVIRONMENTALLY IN CANADA. CANADA IS GOING TO FACE IT WEATHER WISE.

I had more dreams, but I am going to leave them alone because this dream had to do with game play – elimination. So yes, more people are going to be eliminated like game play because, humans' value not life here on Earth.

I will not worry about the soul of humans because, the *SOUL OF HUMANS IS TRULY NOT MY CONCERN. EVERY HUMAN IS ACCOUNTABLE FOR THEIR OWN SOUL. Africa is calling me, and I have to find a way to get to South Africa. I do not know if I have to do something there, or if there is something there for me to learn. All in all, I have to get to South Africa.*

Michelle

I do not know what is going on now in my dream world. I am not sure if the White Race based on hue and excluding the Blacks that fall under the White Banner of Death is going to start war.

I can't get this White Man standing not in a field but at the edge of a field if that is the right way to describe it looking at me. I am so not going to worry about the White Race based on hue and evil deeds because, *YOU KNOW THEY ARE EVIL.* Yes, I am generalizing but it is what it is.

GOOD CANNOT COME FROM EVIL.
EVIL COME FROM EVIL.

As for the Earth I do not know if there is going to be more erosion of lands apart from what I told you above. *As for Israel, I cannot tell you what is going to happen there; if Israel is going to be destroyed.*

Trust me, if Israel thinks God is pleased with them, they had truly better think again. Thus, Revelations of their Bible told you, "WOE BE UNTO THE JEWS THAT CALL THEMSELVES JEWS BECAUSE THEY ARE OF THE SYNAGOGUE OF SATAN."

So, however Israel is destroyed would be due to them because, it was "WHITE JEWS" that "LIED ON GOD, AND DECEIVED NATIONS."

Did I dream me planting roses?

Yes

The soil was dry, and I was uprooting the plants and replanting them. So yes, I know what this dream means, and I am going to leave it alone. I will forever have disappointment in my life when it comes to these books but it's life for me. Many will think I am radical, racist, hate White People, and more from what I write. This is your opinion, and you are entitled to your views and opinion.

Did I dream about going to the doctor?

Yes, and this morning my doctor's office called to book a phone conversation with my doctor. But he need not call because I know what the conversation entails. Yes, his concern about my health yada, yada, yada.

I need to get back to taking care of me. My muscle spasms are acting up again, but I know that my body is lacking the vitamins and minerals that are key to my body.

Cleaned, walked my dogs, ate, and now I am going back to bed to play my games. Truly do not feel like writing. So, I write a little then stop.

Michelle
May 12, 2021

Lovey, despite you asking me to write you a book; *why is it so hard for me?*

Am I your Chosen?

Now tell me Lovey. Why is it that humans tarnish you despite all you've done for us here on Earth and in the Spiritual Realm?

Why is it the battle here on Earth is so hard to overcome when it comes to evil; every facet of wickedness and evil?

Why is it so easy to fall for evil Lovey?

Now tell me Lovey, why is it so hard for Black People to break the chains of evil?

Why is evil so lucrative for so many Lovey?

Why is it that *YOU ARE NOT CHOSEN LOVEY BY EVERY HUMAN HERE ON EARTH?*

Have we forgotten life, and what life truly mean?
Have we forgotten life, and what life is truly about?

Now Lovey tell me. If "the wages of sin is death;" why would you sin – die for humans by breaking your own laws?

According to the Bible of Man – White Man – man's so called Holy Bible. YOU SINNED.

YOU TOLD YOUR PROPHETS TO SIN – KILL.

Now tell me. *ARE YOU NOT DISOBEDIENT?*

DID YOU NOT KNOWINGLY AND WILLINGLY BREAK YOUR OWN LAWS – COMMANDMENTS WITH YOUR PROPHETS?

Now tell me Lovey. *HOW ARE YOU OF LIFE WHEN YOU TOO HAVE SINNED – WILLINGLY AND KNOWINGLY BREAK YOUR OWN LAWS – COMMANDMENTS AS WRITTEN BY MEN, SO-CALLED WHITE JEWS?*

Yes, Satan's true own. Thus, demons walk and live amongst us period.

Now tell me Lovey. *DO YOU NOT HAVE A SIN RECORD IF YOU BREAK YOUR OWN LAWS – COMMANDMENTS?*

ARE YOU NOT GOING TO DIE LIKE MAN – THE WICKED AND EVIL OF EARTH AND THE SPIRITUAL REALM?

DOES DEATH NOT HAVE YOU LOCKED IN HELL FOR DISOBEYING YOUR OWN LAWS – COMMANDMENTS?

Now tell me. *HOW CAN TRUTH SIN?*

HOW CAN TRUTH LIE?

HOW CAN TRUTH DISOBEY LIFE?

Lovey, you sinned according to man – White Jews thus, Death own you period. See, man's Holy Bible Lovey.

So now tell me. *If God cannot obey his own laws – commandments, how can man – humans?*

Therefore, I cannot cry for the wicked and evil Lovey you know this, but with what's happening here on Earth, I have to wonder about Black People on a whole.

There is a life to be had yet, we believe in lies when it comes to you Lovey. Lies that take us from you Lovey come on now.

When we believe in lies, do you not move further from us?

Now let me ask you this; *WHY DID YOU ALLOW THE BIBLE OF MAN TO BE WRITTEN?*

I KNOW THE BIBLE IS NOT OF YOU, BUT BILLIONS BELIEVE IT'S YOU THUS, MAKING YOU A MONSTER. But Lovey, WHY DID YOU NOT SHUT THE WHITE RACE OF EVIL DOWN FROM WRITING THIS BOOK?

Why allow billions to belief in this lie Lovey?

Why permit this book – the Bible of Man to be written?

The Bible of Man – White Race did deceive billions Lovey. Billions are going to die Spiritually for their believe in this book; man's so called Holy Bible.

Lovey, many did go to their grave already believing in the Book; Bible of Man – the White Race.

I grew up believing in the lie but then, the Church was never for me. I did not, and do not conform to their beliefs of *DYING TO ATTAIN LIFE, AND MORE*. Plus, *WHEN YOU HAVE A GIFT; THE GIFT OF LIFE, MANY TRULY DO NOT LIKE YOU.*

Many things we are taught yet, none has and have looked into the lies of the Bible when it comes to you Lovey why?

Why is it that *the LIE OF THE WHITE RACE IS SO PERFECT THAT IT TOOK BILLIONS FROM YOU – LIFE LOVEY?*

Why can't humans learn that the *PRICE OF SIN IS DEATH* once the Spirit shed the Flesh?

Now tell me, *WHAT CHANGES DO YOU WANT AND NEED FOR YOURSELF HERE ON EARTH LOVEY?*

WHAT DO YOU SEE FOR YOURSELF WHEN IT COMES TO HUMANS ON A WHOLE, IF YOU THINK ANYTHING AT ALL OF HUMANS?

Yes, the damage is done here on Earth and it's sad that life have to be this way, but it's what it is I guess. We cannot change the past and now of the way things are. Many humans truly do not want to change because the life they are living suit them just fine and that's fine. Life is truly not for all thus, Death. But Lovey, _WHY IS THE PHYSICAL SO IMPORTANT FOR BILLIONS?_

Meaning, why do humans not think of their _SPIRITUAL WELL BEING – LIFE?_

Why is it that we neglect the spirit – you Lovey?

Maybe I am overthinking too much but, truly thank you Lovey for being the good and true you you are. You did segregate yourself from all evil thus, you had to leave out of Earth due to the unclean nature of humans. So yes, you did do good by you and for you in this way. Yes, it's sad that humans are truly not waking up and seeing what is going on around them and what is going to happen to billions shortly.

I cannot think of the wicked and evil Lovey. I have to do all to secure me and my life with you not just for myself but for the seeds you've given me, and those who are truly true and dear to me.

Yes, it's hard here on Earth. I do not have a portal to walk to you as I am and in my walking to you, you are cleansing my Physical and Spiritual Well Being and DNA.

Energy and Time for me eludes me. I do not have the proper speed and vibration to connect to you and the great energy that is out there. Yes, it's sad when you do not have the proper knowledge you need to achieve certain things with you Lovey.

Too bad you could not sit with me via my dream world for us to reason properly.

Aye Lovey because Earth has been used and abused by humans. Now tell me Lovey; why does she continue to take the abuse?

Now Lovey, do people – humans not know that there is a SPIRITUAL LIFE AND DEATH TO BE HAD?

And I am not going to go any further. Many truly do not think of their Spiritual Life.

THE LIES OF THE BIBLE DID DECEIVE BILLIONS literally Lovey. Many truly do not know their hell in Hell for real.

Why give up life for Death?
Why are we so deceived Lovey?

Why do people have to live in deceit because of one race, and the different races?

What profit can you have in Death apart from death; the death of flesh and spirit?

I don't want to think right now Lovey so, I am going to lay down and play my game. Right now Lovey, all I want and need is for you to be truly there for me. I can't walk away from you. Despite me wanting and needing a break from writing, I am still writing. So yes, I am glued to you in some way.

Lovey, *THE BOOK OF GOOD AND EVIL.*

Just as you have your book Lovey, Evil hath their book also. Yes, the Bible of Man is the BOOK OF EVIL FOR WHICH I CALL DEATH'S BOOK.

Hopefully soon Lovey you will permit me to see into your realm of goodness and truth – life.

Michelle
May 12, 2021

Now tell me Lovey, why do people – humans and spirit not worry about their Spiritual Life?

Why do some wait until the last minute; when they are dead, and they see and know their penalty – *TIME IN HELL* they are reaching out to me?

I can't save them. I know not them. I know Hell is truly not pretty but then; *SINS ARE TRULY NOT PRETTY BUT UGLY – TRULY BLACK AND UGLY.*

Wow because now I am thinking of DMX. Did I dream see his grave recently?

I believe I did. I do not know if it's because I was seeing something to do with his funeral and burial spot on YouTube. I did not watch it but trust me, he was shut down immediately from reaching out to me. *Certain sins there are no remission and or, forgiveness of sins. If you have sold your soul, made sacrifices unto Death, go against all the laws of life, then you cannot be saved. It makes no sense to reach out to me in Death because; DEATH WILL SHUT YOU DOWN, AND I WILL SHUT YOU DOWN.*

Your life and life's worth should not come down to money, fame, selling your soul, disrespecting THE GOD OF TRUTH AND LIFE, whoredom, shutting you and your family including children out of life – THE REALM OF GOD.

DEATH PROTECT LIFE THUS, IT'S DEATH THAT ENSURE ALL WHO ARE WICKED AND EVIL CANNOT ATTAIN LIFE; A LIFE OF TRUTH AND GOODNESS WITH GOD.

YOUR SINS ARE YOUR DEATH RECORD. Thus, EACH SIN COME WITH A DEATH PENALTY; COST TO YOUR SPIRIT.

I truly do not need to know the hell of some dead. BILLIONS HERE ON EARTH TRULY DO NOT THINK OF THEIR LIFE AFTER DEATH. And, I cannot think of it for them. THERE IS LIFE AFTER THE FLESH IS GONE. Thus, the Physical and Spiritual are separated, and there is A SPIRITUL LIFE AND A SPIRITUAL DEATH. Therefore, it's imperative you know the TRUTH OF LIFE AND DEATH.

Many things are put on God, but there are many things God cannot do. There are no penalties to life however, there are penalties to Death; THE SINS YOU DO DAY IN AND DAY OUT.

Life is not what religion, and your religious leaders tell you it is. *Life is what and how you make it.*

Life is not about hate and strife.

Life is not about self hate and hating others.
Life is not complex though at times we say it is.

Life is not dirty. Life is clean.

Life is not loud therefore, practice silence at times.

Life is not worldly therefore, strive to live simple and stress free.

Life is within therefore, do the good you can to live within, with others, and with God.

Think of your life and where you want to be. Absolutely no one can protect your life but you. Yes, there are saved in life, and a saved in life can save you thus, *THOSE WHO ARE OF LIFE MUST DO ALL TO PROTECT SELF, AND THE CHILDREN AND PEOPLE OF GOD – GOOD AND TRUE LIFE.*

Goodness cannot save Evil because there is absolutely no goodness in Evil.

Yes, many people live to kill here on Earth. That is their job. The more they kill is the more they rack up time in Hell; the hell they created for self here on Earth. And yes, the more they kill is the further God move away from humans here on Earth.

THEREFORE, EVIL DIRTY ALL.

EVIL CANNOT BE CLEAN.
EVIL CANNOT MAINTAIN CLEANLINESS.

EVIL CANNOT BE FAIR AND JUST.
EVIL MUST LIE AND DO LIE.

EVIL KILL THUS, EARTH HAS AND HAVE BECOME THE DOMAIN OF DEATH – PHYSICAL DEATH.

Listen, there is a lot of negativity around us.

We speak negative things.

People say negative things about you.
You say negative things about you.
You say negative things about others.

What can you do?

There are days when you are all out negative. Lord have mercy do I know this because I talk about my negative days in these books. Yes, it would be nice to vent, and I do. My venting is with God. God is my go too source for venting.

Listen, I do not have the privilege to have friends or true friends apart from God, my true guides, and some of my family members. That's about it for me. But for my negative days; God is my true go too source. Lord have mercy to the way I vent with God I have to wonder if God has Michelle Venting Days because, I wear God out. I have to. When you have truth and doubt, and you trust God that much then you will comprehend what I am talking about. Therefore, GOD IS GOOD ALL THE TIME despite the way I write on some days, question God, blast God, doubt God, and so much more.

Listen everyone, God has and have been trying, it is us as individuals THAT WANT GOD TO DO WHAT GOD CANNOT DO.

God do give to us; help up. It is us as humans that cannot be satisfied.

God is there for us, it is us that believe in lies when it comes to God then expect God to help us given the lies we accept and believe in.

If you know that God is right, why do you say God is wrong?

I do when I am having a bad day. At times I want to leave, but leave and go where? I know what Hell is all about, and I truly do not want to go there.

Listen, IF RELIGION WAS/IS RIGHT, GOD WOULD NOT HAVE A PROBLEM WITH RELIGION. And Lovey, if I am wrong in saying *this; please let me know because, I know for a fact without doubt you have absolutely nothing to do with Religion.*

Religion is a lie.
Religion is dirty.
Religion makes you dirty.
Religion is of death.
Religion take(s) you to hell.
Religion defy life.

Religion causes you to lose your soul and life.

Religion is money; profit and prophet for those who use Religion to lie and deceive.

No Religion is ordained by God. God do not deal in nastiness, lies, deceit, death, and more.

Religion paint God as inept.
Dirty

Love and truly love all that is nasty and unclean.

Religion paint God as a warmonger.

A thief
Murderer
Incest loving god
Confused
Delusional
Negative
All out evil, and more.

So now tell me, how can God save anyone when we believe God is nasty; unclean?

Is God a Demon?

Why would God say this, this, and this, then go back on his or her word and tell you to disobey the order you were given to follow?

Is God a giver backer taker?
Is God a liar and deceiver like humans?

As humans we truly do not sit down and reflect on our life and our life with God.

We do not look into the _LIES OF THE BIBLES OF MEN._

We do not question therefore, we've become accepting of lies and deceit.

IF SOMETHING IS KILLING YOU THEN THAT SOMETHING IS TRULY NOT RIGHT FOR YOU.

Why stay with or in negative situations? Find a better way out come on now.

Listen:
EVIL ABUSE
EVIL IS DEATH

EVIL CANNOT BE FAIR
EVIL CANNOT BE JUST
EVIL CANNOT BE RIGHT
EVIL CONQUER
EVIL DOMINATE
EVIL SIN
EVIL IS SIN

So why stay with evil?

<u>If God is protecting you. Stay protected. Do not give up your life for naught because; "THE LIFE WE LIVE HERE ON EARTH IS TRULY NOT ALL."</u>

<u>"THE LIFE WE LIVE HERE ON EARTH DETERMINE(S) WHERE WE GO ONCE THE SPIRIT SHED THE FLESH."</u>

<u>THERE IS LIFE OR DEATH TO BE HAD ONCE YOUR SPIRIT SHED THE FLESH.</u> And, if your life is truly not right here on Earth, how are you going to be saved by God?

If God know you not; how can God save you?

GOD IS NOT A TRAP.

EVIL IS A TRAP BECAUSE, EVIL TRAP YOU TO DEATH AND HELL. There are no ands, ifs, or buts about this. You know this.

Now Lovey, let me ask you this. *WHERE DID YOU GO?*

WHY IS IT SO HARD TO FIND YOU SPIRITUALLY AND EARTHLY?

HOW DID YOU ESCAPE EARTH?

WHAT PATHWAY AND OR, GATEWAY DID YOU TAKE TO GET OUT OF EARTH?

I KNOW LIFE CANNOT DIE, AND YOU DID NOT DIE, SO WHAT TRANSPORT DID YOU USE IF ANY TO LEAVE EARTH?

I know gravity, and the use of energy as a mode of transport, but you literally disappeared from Earth.

How and or, how come you can leave Earth just like that without anyone knowing and I cannot?

I don't know if I am on the right path Lovey, but I had to ask because I need a path and or, road, and or, pathway out of Earth without shedding the flesh, and it's impossible for me because; I am extremely limited *ENERGY WISE.* There is so much to know and learn when it comes to Energy, and I cannot attain this knowledge.

Is there a formula to energy that I can use Lovey?

Is there a formula to energy that no one knows of?

No, that was a stupid question Michelle. No one knows of this formula here on Earth. If we did, we would be able to use it and leave out of Earth at will.

But Lovey, <u>EVIL HAS THIS FORMULA BECAUSE EVIL DO HAVE ACCESS TO EARTH.</u> But Evil do not have access to Lovey's domain Michelle.

You know what Lovey, it is confusing. Thinking of the key – gateway to life; you Lovey is hurting my head. Certain knowledge I have no access to, and you are truly not letting me know.

I do not want my mind to perceive when it comes to you Lovey. I need to see you as you are face to face. Therefore, I need you to lift that veil from over my eyes when it comes to you. I need that purity where I can see you and your world clearly with the eyes that I have, but you are truly not letting me in Lovey; why?

It's hard for me Lovey because many questions I have.

No Lovey, how did you leave out of Earth?

I need to know the truth. Yes, I want to leave out of Earth with my flesh without having to have to face death. Yet, this knowledge I cannot access.

Yes, with this knowledge I know I would be able to find you, but do you not want and need this for me Lovey?

Do you not want me to find you as I am truthfully Lovey?

Am I overstepping my place with you in this sense Lovey?

Do you not crave me to the point where you want me in your domain now without restrictions?

Yes, crazy me, but am I crazy in that sense in wanting and seeking the true truth from you when it comes to Life and you as well as, life with you and me?

Energy is a key to life.

So now Lovey. How do you access this energy and use it?

There is something I am truly missing when it comes to energy.

Lovey, I need knowledge.

There has to be an opening when it comes to knowledge.

You can bend gravity. Therefore, you can use energy to access your realm Lovey but that knowledge I do not have.

Wow

I know I am on the right path but getting there; access to life; you Lovey is truly hard.

Why do you have to make me find Lovey? Meaning, make it so difficult for me to find. The knowledge I have many truly do not have this I know, but this final step; journey to you Lovey, you are keeping from me; why?

I know Earth is not clean, but LIFE IS NOT DEPENDENT ON THE FLESH. LIFE REQUIRES THE SPIRIT. THEREFORE, LIFE IS DEPENDENT ON THE SPIRIT – THAT ENERGY INSIDE OF YOU.

Our Spirit is our Life Source.
Our Spirit is our Electricity.
Charge.

But in knowing this, I am missing so much Lovey; why?

Now tell me, why is it that the Black Race have to be the eliminated race?

Why is it so hard for Africans to tell the truth?

Knowledge is one of the keys to life Lovey yet, we as humans are truly not knowledgeable; why?

Yes, we lost all contact with you thus, the knowledge we as humans need to know, we truly do not know nor can attain?

Sad yes, but isn't this the way things were set up when we fell from grace? Meaning, gave up our life for death.

The basics we do not have Lovey because humans live to kill and do kill. We've become warped believers and not true knowers of the truth; why?

And if I am wrong in saying this tell me I am wrong Lovey and truly forgive me.

Now tell me Lovey. *WHAT HOPE CAN ANYONE FIND IN MISERY?*

Now tell me Lovey. Why is it that the White Race want dominion over Earth?

Do they not know that no Race can have dominion of and over Earth?

The Flesh cannot conquer the Spirit period. Therefore, every human that has more Sin than Good must go to Hell; the hell they created for self and die.

Tell me Lovey. Why do the White Race want control of everything to the point of lying and killing to get their desire here on Earth?

Now Lovey why…no, let me leave it because as Black People; WE TOO ARE TO BE BLAMED FOR WHAT IS HAPPENING TO US HERE ON EARTH. I will not be a hypocrite when it comes to things. We as Black People can make better choices for self but with the false and brainwashed education we've accepted and pass on to our children and future generations, many cannot change.

Many will still be looking for goodness in evil when ABSOLUTELY NO ONE CAN FIND GOODNESS IN EVIL.

What can I say to you Lovey?

My body is getting tired, and I am feeling sleepy.

After writing that yesterday it's May 15, 2021 and I cannot go back to sleep to my dream Lovey. It's 4:39 am and now I am writing though I did not want to get up and write.

Now let me ask you this Lovey.

WHY AM I SEEING MORE AND MORE OF BABYLON, AND THE PEOPLE OF BABYLON?

I truly do not want or need to connect with Babylon in that way, but I guess I can't get around them. Nasty are they from my dream.

Oh god Allelujah for real.

Dreamt I was in the home of someone I know. He's of Pakistani descent and he's my daughter's friend.

I was in his home and there was this older Babylonian Man in the dream. Elder for clarity. I cannot tell you what he was dressed in because I was not noticing his dress. He wanted water and I told him I would get it for him. He gave me his glass and I asked him if he wanted ice in the water. He said something to me about giving him ice in the water. It was as if he could not believe I would put ice in his water to drink.

I wanted to ask him about giving him tap water but did not. He got up from where he was, and I followed him. He had 3 staffs with him, and he put the staffs in like a umbrella rack. One staff I know is of Sikh writing. I checked Google and the sign is of the Om Symbol without the 3 and accent. The other I think is of Gemini, and the other I cannot remember.

Checking Google, the Gemini Sign is not it, but the staff had two lines with a curve at the top if I can remember correctly and Lovey forgive me if I am wrong because, I cannot fully remember the second and third symbol.

Going into the kitchen to wash the glass, the glass was nasty, and I did not want to wash it because something was on the outside of the glass that revolted me; made me want to gag. I washed the glass anyway with green liquid soap. And even writing about the glass makes me want to gag literally. When you think of drinking glass think a Mason Jar without the handle and or, Round Economy Jar. Washing the glass, you could see that he had not washed his glass in a while because I had to clean the brown rust that was in the glass.

Washing the glass, I was not washing this straw basket; the top of this basket. It was dirty but I managed to wash it clean. Washing the basket, it was like it was going to fall apart but it did not fall apart. After washing the basket and glass jar his young nephew and or, relative said when he wanted to make clothing; no, not clothing but wrap I believe to let him help me, and I should cut the cloth from the cloth in the window; window curtain. He would be there. See I was using a brown material to wash the basket and at the end, I was trying to fold the material but could not fold it. It was tall and ripped at the end.

Suffice it to say, I did not give the old man – elder his water with ice. The scene changed with Thalia coming into the dream and she was telling him, the old man's nephew and or, relative she could get him a job at her workplace. She was telling him about the job, and she referenced computers and he said something. I had to chime in and tell Thalia that he was a computer programmer, and he designed the system at her workplace. I also asked him about Jennoy. Jennoy was also a programmer that I knew.

I will not analyze this dream because I know what the dream means, and I don't know.

Now Lovey, let me ask you this.

<u>WHY AM I TASKED IN CLEANING THE NASTINESS OF BABYLON?</u>

<u>Have Babylon not hurt, and raped the Black Race enough?</u>

<u>Have Babylon not caused many in Africa to stray and marry into their fold knowing full well it was, and is still forbidden for BLACKS TO MARRY THE CHILDREN AND PEOPLE OF BABYLON?</u>

Have the Children and People of Babylon not caused many in Africa to die in the days of old?

So, why is Africans not telling the truth of what Babylon did to Blacks in the days of old?

Thus, all of Babylon was and still is locked out of life literally Lovey.

And none of you better come to me with colour or call me racist. You cannot go back in time like I can thus, my dream world.

Listen, THIS HAS NOTHING TO DO WITH COLOUR OF SKIN BUT LIFE – GOD. THE GOD AND GODS OF BABYLON ARE TRULY NOT OF LIFE THEREFORE, THE CHILDREN OF LIFE WERE AND IS STILL FORBIDDEN TO MARRY THE CHILDREN AND PEOPLE OF BABYLON UNTIL THIS DAY.

Many Africans did marry the Children and People of Babylon thus MIXED RACE BLACKS AND INDIANS.

LOVEY GO BACK TO THE LIONS AND WHAT BABYLON DID TO THE LIONS, LYONS, LYON BACK IN THE DAYS OF OLD. SO WHY THE HELL SHOULD I CLEAN UP BABYLON WHEN YOU HAVE ABSOLUTELY NOTHING TO DO WITH BABYLON AND THE CHILDREN OF BABYLON?

Come on Lovey. ALL OF BABYLON INCLUDING MIXED RACE BABYLONIANS ARE LOCKED OUT OF LIFE, AND I AM TO OPEN THE GATE FOR THEM!!!

I am not stupid because you see and know the nastiness of them; Babylon. The lockout stays. Yes, I have to remember goodness and I do, but I truly cannot open that door. I refuse to. You Lovey have to keep that door closed.

Now, if you Lovey want to open your door to Babylon, you do it on your accord. I will not stand with you on this one. Dem nuh like wi period.

It is not just Black People that have and has followed in the path and pathway of Babylon. Many Whites did. Just look at Russia, and I am going to leave it there because many truly do not know the truth period. Many do not know that the Russian Empire is rooted in Babylon.

So now tell me Lovey. IS BABYLON GOING TO TAKE CONTROL OF EARTH AGAIN UNDER THE QUIET AND UNBENOUNCED TO THE WHITE RACE GLOBALLY?

Technology Lovey and my dream that I wrote about in I NEED ANSWERS GOD PART THREE with the Babylonian Indians that went into space, and what he told me at the end of the dream.

In regards to technology Lovey, what new technology do the Children and People of Babylon has and have developed under the quiet that people do not know about?

Lovey, are the Children and People of Babylon going to use their computer skills and knowledge to wipe out people's bank account globally including Corporate Bank Accounts?

Lovey, I cannot fully analyze this dream because I truly do not know what these 3 staffs represent. Nor do I know why the old man was surprised I would give him water with ice.

Now, is this Hell from Hell on a different level Lovey?

So now tell me Lovey. What is going to happen to Pakistan, India, Italy, Canada, Russia, Asian and European Lands on a whole?

Lovey, Babylon cannot take control of Earth again come on now. You know just how destructive and nasty these people are. They truly do not like Black People and it's time we as Black People wake up and know the full and true truth.

Africa and Africans have to wake up and tell the truth if they can because You and I know Africa and Africans did sell you out Lovey. Thus, their tribal warfare, religious lies, polygamy of nastiness, them; Africans that truly do not know who and what they are literally.

No Lovey, I am sick and tired of the *LIES AFRICA AND AFRICANS KEEP ALL AROUND. YOU CANNOT CONTINUE TO KEEP BLACKS TRAPPED TO LIES; DEATH.*

Many Africans did sell out thus Slavery come on now.

So, when it comes to Canada, India, Pakistan, Italy, I truly do not know. Whatever death is coming to these lands is truly up to Death and in a way, I truly do not want to know. <u>All I know right now is that CANADA IS GOING TO BURN.</u> So which provinces I truly do not know. All I know is, I could not get over the smell of fire when it comes to Canada.

I will not worry about Canada because Canada is no longer clean, and this land must face the consequences of their evil actions. This the People of Canada can thank their inept and unclean leaders for.

<u>WHEN YOU OPEN UP YOUR LAND AND LANDS TO DEATH, DEATH DO CONSUME YOUR LAND.</u>

Death and the Children and People of Death do destroy your land, and the people of the/your land.

<u>ABSOLUTELY NO ONE CAN GET LIFE FROM DEATH. ALL YOU GET IS DEATH.</u>

So yes, the crap of dung facing the globe war wise, strife wise, hate wise, and more is going to resonate here in Canada. Thus Lovey, <u>I need to get out of Canada; NORTH AMERICAN LANDS because; there is absolutely no saving grace for NORTH AMERICAN LANDS IN MY VIEW.</u>

And in truth, I truly don't want North American Lands to have or get a Saving Grace from you Lovey. And no, I will not save North America if I am tasked with saving lands.

Come now Lovey. I can't keep telling you I need an escape from this land, and you are truly not listening to me or hearing me. You keep me shackled and chained to hell; the land I am in thus, causing me dire unhappiness and sin. When you keep me in a land I truly do not want or need to be in, you Lovey do not respect me or truly care about me.

Canada is going to burn. You know Earth is going to burn yet, I am not safely in the land you truly need me to be in so that we can begin our new life together.

No, I will not cry for NORTH AMERICAN LANDS BECAUSE, I KNOW I CAN TAKE THE BONES OF MY MOTHER OUT WITHOUT PENALTY, AND THIS; TAKING THE BONES OF MY MOTHER OUT OF NORTH AMERICA I TRULY NEED TO DO.

THE CHILDREN AND PEOPLE OF LIFE CAN NO LONGER BE BURIED IN THE CEMETERIES OF DEATH. When we continue to do this, we are forsaking our life Lovey come on now.

<u>*WE CANNOT HAVE TRUTH LIVING AMONGST DEATH COME ON NOW.*</u>

You know that which is right Lovey therefore, we need to do that which is right for us and our good and true own. I will not save North American Lands because North American Lands is truly not for me to save in my view.

I will not save Babylonian Lands because Babylon is truly not for me to save. You did lock out all of Babylon from your world Lovey and I have to respect you. I cannot petition you to save Babylon. Like I said, I have to remember goodness. I cannot forget goodness those Babylonians that has and have done goodness for me. Nor can I forget the past of the Lions, Lyon, Lyons and what the Children and People of Babylon did to them. This I cannot forgive Lovey come on now, and I will never ever forgive.

So, what death is coming to Earth from Space, the Sky, Beyond the Realm of Life, I truly do not know. All I know is, the heavens; sky is gearing up for war; death. The Time of Death is up Lovey. Truly let it be up and let's take our children and people to safety where they do not have to hear the cries and pain of billions. <u>*Thus, I asked you; how did you escape Earth?*</u>

Our Children and People need this escape Lovey. <u>You are our PORTAL OF LIFE</u> therefore we need to know how to escape this judgement that is *coming. A judgement that is going to see billions lose their life. If it was not so Lovey, then you would not have given me SEEDS TO PLANT OVER 100 MILLION ACRES.*

Thus, I need GROWTH; TRUE GROWTH, TRUE TRUTH AND GOODNESS, TRUE PEACE, TRUE HARMONY, TRUE LIFE AND PROSPERITY, TRUE LOVE, TRUE BALANCE, AND MORE GOOD AND TRUE THINGS FOR OUR GOOD AND TRUE OWN ONLY LOVEY.

I cannot come to you Lovey for all who are not of life because; all who are not of life is/are not our children and people; of life period. You Lovey cannot keep our people amongst Death's own because, DEATH MUST CONSUME EARTH SHORTLY.

You know I am not a last minute person Lovey come on now. So, please let the Exodus start for our good and true own only.

Billions did not secure their life with you Lovey and I truly cannot worry about billions. I have to safeguard our good and true own, and ensure that they are safe; reach your home safely, but I cannot do this without you Lovey come on now.

Yes, there is so much for me to learn but I cannot learn without your good and true help Lovey. Right now, you are showing me Babylon, but I truly do not want or need to have anything to do with Babylon. They are truly not our children and people.

PEOPLE THAT NEED LIFE DO ALL THAT THEY CAN GOOD AND TRUE TO MAINTAIN AND SUSTAIN THEIR LIFE WITH YOU AND IN YOU LOVEY COME ON NOW.

You do not go out of your way to destroy Blacks. It's not right. Therefore, we as Black People need to change our way of thinking, clothing, doing business, the way we raise our children, the way we educate self and each other, what we eat, what we drink, how we pray – talk to you Lovey, and more.

I am going to go back to bed because my left eye is bothering me but, before I go. *What changes are their when it comes to tattoos Lovey if any?*

Please let me know so that I can inform our Children and People. *Therefore Lovey, our Children and People must not accept the Brand and Brands of Death. Absolutely no branded – tattooed freaks of any kind in our land or lands Lovey.*

The Mark and Marks of the Beast stay with Death – Satan and all who have and has accepted Death physically and spiritually.

Michelle

Slept and I dreamt my disk and or, crazier broke. I have to get another one and back up the one I am using now.

Now Lovey. We know why Babylon is excluded out of life. Now, the White Race is excluded out of life therefore, NO RETURN.

Now, why can't the different races including some of our own Blacks realize to; *LEAVE BLACK PEOPLE ALONE. WE DO NOT BOTHER YOU, TRULY DON'T BOTHER US. WHEN YOU MESS WITH US; THOSE WHO ARE OF TRUE PEACE YOU WILL LOSE YOUR LIFE ALL AROUND.*

Babylon learnt this the hard way. Now the White Race will learn this the hard way also.

Lovey, we cannot give life unto Death. Meaning, the Job of Death is to take who belong to Death therefore, it stops now with the killing of our good and true own. We can no longer be sacrifices unto death therefore, we must be separated and segregated from Death's wicked and evil own.

We can no longer die amongst Death's Own.

We can no longer bury the flesh of our Children and People amongst Death's Own.

We can no longer support Death's Wicked and Evil Own.

*We have to protect our good and true life and place with you
Lovey come on now.*

*What is so wrong with Black People that every race do all to
deceive us, lie to us, destroy and kill us?*

No Lovey, I can't keep asking the same questions over
and over again with you. We have to do something in
truth to truly help our good and true own.

I just ate and my body is truly not right.

I so need to go lay down Lovey.

Until later.

Michelle

DON'T YOU TROUBLE ZION

I wish I could find the right person on YouTube that could sing and represent this song the way it was meant to be sung; represented. Yes, Revival Time the Zionist Way stomping and banding the right and proper way.

SEE BABYLON AND THE WHITE RACE DID NOT GET THE MEMO NOT TO TROUBLE ZION – GOD BECAUSE, WHEN GOD STRIKE BACK THAT STRIKING BACK IS YOU BEING MORE THAN INFINITELY AND INDEFINITELY BEING LOCKED OUT OF LIFE – THE WORLD AND LIFE OF GOD PERIOD.

You do not lie on God.
You do not lie on the Children and People of God.

You do not do all to take the Children and People of Life from God.

You do not do all to discredit God and the Children and People of Life – God.

You do not do all to dirty the Children and People of Life including, the Land and Lands of the Children and People of Life.

You do not do all to turn the Children and People of Life – God against God.

You do not do all to kill the Children and People of God.

You do not lie on any form or Life whether Physical or Spiritual.

<u>*Life is pivotal.*</u> *You do not lose it. Meaning, you do not lie on life, you will not like the consequences.*

So no, <u>ONE RACE CANNOT CONTROL THE WORLD.</u>

You know total control is what the Demons of Hell want and need here on Earth Lovey thus, the Children and People they control, tell what to do in the form of death Lovey. Therefore, we cannot allow our Children and People to fall under the rulership of Evil again.

<u>*BLACK PEOPLE LISTEN AND LISTEN TO ME GOOD.*</u>

<u>*IF YOU THINK THE SLAVERY YOUR ANCESTORS AND SOME OF YOU ARE GOING THROUGH RIGHT NOW, YOU TRULY DO NOT KNOW HELL – THE SLAVERY YOU WILL FALL UNDER IF ONE NATION TAKE CONTROL OF EARTH.*</u> *Man's New World Order.*

Trust me, <u>MANY WILL BE ELIMINATED WITHOUT CAUSE BECAUSE, THIS IS WHAT EVIL DO. EVIL ELIMINATE – KILL.</u> Once you have one <u>WORLD ORDER</u> all that you see now; these lock downs, them telling you what you can buy from what you cannot buy, them telling you when you can go out from when you cannot go out, them forcing their medications of death on you at will, them taking away your fundamental human rights from you, them killing you, them telling you when you can go to school, when you can go to the doctor, when to worship your god, and more is nothing compared to what is going to happen to you shortly <u>if THE WHITE RACE AND BABYLON GET FULL AND TOTAL CONTROL OF EARTH.</u>

And don't look at your Leaders, and Black Leaders because; they will be eliminated. None have a say. <u>They have to comply with the "NEW WORLD ORDER OF MEN; SATAN'S CHILDREN AND PEOPLE."</u>

You as humans are the ones who are truly not seeing what's going on around you.

You will have absolutely no say on who lives and who dies because; <u>NOT ONE HUMAN GLOBALLY WILL BE SAFE. THEREFORE, BILLIONS HAVE NO RIGHT OR RIGHTS TO LIFE TO WHAT IS GOING ON NOW, AND WHAT WILL HAPPEN FUTURE WISE.</u> This is why I petition Lovey for the good and true alone. I have to choose right and true for the good and true of life and yes, THE TRULY TRYING TO BE GOOD.

The Laws of Men are not just.

Black People wake up because, you are the target and eliminated race. <u>THE RICH AND FEW THAT RUN THIS WORLD IS TRULY NOT THINKING OF YOU AND THOSE WHO ARE NOT RICH. THEY ARE ONLY THINKING OF THEM AND SURVIVING WHAT IS TO COME SO THAT THEY CAN REBUILD AGAIN FOR THEM.</u>

We as Black People are not safe. We have to collectively come together and provide a safe haven for us.

Listen, to my dream this morning May 18, 2021, Mental Issues in the Black Community is on the rise here in Canada.

Mental Issues in the Babylonian Community is on the rise here in Canada.

Soon we will have no freedom – absolutely no rights if one nation take control and they are taking control. Look and see the damage of their Covid-19 scam – lie. You infected yourself wearing the mask day in and day out.

So now tell me. How can God help us when we continually allow others to take our rights and freedom from us in the name of Politicians – our government leaders, Corporations, Religious Leaders, Gang Leaders, and more.

Your life hath no worth and I am tired of telling you this and unnu naah learn. GAD A PROTEK UNNU AN UNNU NAAH LISTEN. TIC PAP INNA UNNU EASEHOLE?

No, how much more should God try to wake the lots of you up and you are not listening. You're still killing self, and not preparing for what's to come.

WHITE HISTORY IS NOT BLACK HISTORY. WHITE LIFE IS NOT BLACK LIFE.

WHITE DEATH IS NOT BLACK DEATH BUT BECAUSE OF SIN AND DISOBEDIENCE; WHITE DEATH HAS AND HAVE BECOME DEATH FOR HUNDREDS OF MILLIONS OF BLACKS GLOBALLY.

BLACK EDUCATION IS NOT AND TRULY NOT WHITE EDUCATION.

BLACK KNOWLEDGE IS NOT AND TRULY NOT WHITE KNOWLEDGE.

BLACK CREATION IS NOT AND TRULY NOT WHITE CREATION – DEATH.

OUR BLACK GOD IS NOT AND TRULY NOT WHITE. OUR CREATOR AND GOD IS BLACK AND IT'S TIME WE START REPRESENTING OUR BLACK GOD TRUTHFULLY AS WELL AS, RESPECT OUR BLACK GOD.

THEREFORE,

AS A RACE AND PEOPLE, WE HAVE TO ACCEPT WHO WE ARE AND RESPECT SELF AND EACH OTHER.

As a race and people; WE HAVE TO STOP WANTING WHAT THE WHITE MAN HAS.

THE WHITE RACE HAVE NOT LIFE, THEY HAVE DEATH. SO, WHY CONTINUALLY WANT DEATH FOR SELF, YOUR CHILDREN, AND FUTURE GENERATIONS?

GOD DID NOT ABANDON US AS BLACK PEOPLE. WE AS BLACK PEOPLE

ABANDONED OUR BLACK GOD AND CREATOR.

GOD IS NOT KILLING US AS A RACE AND PEOPLE, IT IS US AS INDIVIDUALS AND A RACE AND PEOPLE THAT ARE KILLING US WITH OUR BELIEFS, THE LIES AND DECEIT WE ACCEPT AS BEING THE TRUTH.

Now let me ask you this Black People.

WHEN DID GOD SAY, YOU COULD NOT COME TO ME AND SPEAK TO ME FOR SELF; YOURSELF?

WHEN DID GOD SAY, BLACK PEOPLE YOU ARE SATAN'S CHILDREN AND PEOPLE?

WHEN DID GOD CLOSE THE DOMAIN OF LIFE TO US; THE BLACK RACE?

DID GOT NOT MAKE US DIFFERENT FROM OUR ENEMIES?

Now, TAKE A LOOK AT YOUR HAIR; YOUR CROWN OF GLORY AND TELL ME DIFFERENTLY. YET, SOME HATE THEIR CROWN OF GOLD AND GLORY; WHY?

No Lovey, I am fed up of how hard you've tried to educate us, teach us, show us, an wi suh dyam dunkya. Wi still naah lisen.

I am tired of telling Black People – everyone to strive not to go to hell.

Black People I am tired of telling you:

"HELL IS FULL OF BLACK PEOPLE AND RECRUITING MORE."

No Lovey come on now. LEAVE THOSE BLACKS WHO DO NOT WANT OR NEED LIFE WITH YOU ALONE. STOP HELPING PEOPLE WHO DON'T WANT YOUR HELP OR YOU.

AS BLACKS WI TOO FOOL, FOOL.

Yes, I went there. Enough is enough now Lovey come on now. Look. Do you think when I am in the land you want and need me in I would leave out? Hell to the no. As long as I am happy, well fed, contented, truly love my home and land, yu caane get mi out.

Do you even think I would share you?

Truss mi, if I had a lock and key to lock you up in my domain so that none can reach you or come near you, I would lock you up an dash wey di key where you cannot find it.

I don't want or need to share you already fi mi fi goh share you again or even let you go all out fi save dunkya people wey caane think about their Physical and Spiritual Life. No sah. Not on my watch. Therefore, end it all now. Stop trying to save people who cannot see, or who do not want to be saved. Leave them to the death they have chosen for self. I keep telling you this and you are truly not listening to me.

Black People nuh respek yu. Suh, wey yu a save dem fa?

Have Blacks not shown you time and time again that they love and truly love the offerings of Death? Thus, Black Lands are littered with the Whorehouses of Death – Churches.

My land, water, waterways, you, portion of Earth, domain, clothing, books, food, life, medicine, sex, talk, walk, breathing, nakedness, shoes, plants, trees of life, fruits, waterfalls, waterspouts, springs, rivers, lakes, seas, and more should not be of the wicked and evil. All must be truly separate. This is our good and true beginning Lovey so why should we not live truly connected, true, truly peaceful, truly war and strife free, truly harmonious, truly balanced, and more good and true things together? I refuse to be separated from you like you are separated from Mother Earth. This is not life for me therefore, our domain must stay and be clean more than forever ever without end come on now. No sickness or death must be in our land and lands; domains come on now.

Why the hell should I want Sin and Death in our world?

We are of true peace Lovey come on now. No, I refuse to share you again. Yes, you can be mad at me all you want but sue me. I am that jealous and so are you.

Look how you've been protecting Black People and still we cannot see this. We keep running back into the fire. I learnt the hard way Lovey, and I refuse the hard way. I refuse to go back to learning the hard way. I am staying protected despite my hurt and pain.

You've shown me hell.
I know hell.
I know the fire that burn the spirit.

Why the hell should I give up truth with you for Death; a worse hell. Strupid plasta ova mi face.

Strupid tattoo pan mi head?

I do not need the offerings of Death.
I do not need the life of Death.

I need the good and true life of life come on now.

No Lovey, you should not have to try so hard with Black People come on now.

Hell is truly not worth it come on now.

Listen, I live in pain. Anna mi fi gi up fimi life fi gaah Hell and face datdey hell. IT IS ONLY A FOOLISH PERSON THAT WOULD GIVE UP THEIR LIFE HERE ON EARTH TO GO TO HELL AND DIE.

This is why I plead with you for goodness Lovey. Yu caane sey mi nuh plead with you for goodness and truth. Look at how much I have bought with you in the name of goodness to give to good and true people. Thus, <u>I NEED MY GOOD GOD AND ALLELUJAH GIVING ROOM IN OUR HOUSE; HOME.</u>

And you better not deny mi this goodness Lovey because you <u>KNOW HOW I TRULY LOVE TO GIVE.</u>

No Lovey, we have to give good and true of each other. I will not settle for anything less. Goodness is beautiful and you know this thus, my goodness is so different. People will not comprehend my goodness but as long as you can Lovey, I am truly good to go. I refuse to give to get come on now.

Yes, I've petitioned you to let one of my good(ness) outweigh all my sins. It is up to you to do this, however, I will not give up on goodness all when I cuss you out and I've told you this. I've told you, no matter how I tell you to leave me alone, and I am leaving you for you not to leave me. Still hold on to me because despite it all, you are all I have on some of my lonely days. I am learning to be satisfied with the little I have. But our house Lovey have to be huge and nice. We have to have our outdoor kitchen, bathroom, and shower area. I will not settle for anything less. I have to be near the waters of life come on now because you know how I truly love water.

Once I know how to create a bed of water. See you Lovey, because I be sleeping on my water. Smile because I know you are getting jealous, but you can join me. We can laugh and talk and have fun.

I know feather light. I need to take more than a ton load of weight off my spirit. There are things I need to do Lovey to truly make me happy and I am hoping you are there with me when I start the change to a more truer and better life with you.

Come on Lovey. *I've had to learn the hard way not to build people who are not true, and you need to learn this lesson as well come on now.* It's not everyone that is of life that are thankful and true. Sometimes I am ungrateful when it comes to you because I am spoilt. Yes, there are days when I truly want and need you to spoil me my way. *But, ARE HUMANS NOT TRULY UNGRATEFUL WHEN IT COMES TO YOU?*

How do you as God handle this ungratefulness?

How do you balance your life?

Lord have mercy do I stress you out. So, I don't think you can balance your life with me and the trouble I give you with my writings; well, these books.

Lovey, do people even know and learn about true thanks and gratitude?

I don't know what this is coming off with the thanks and gratitude, but truly; do people even know and learn about true thanks and gratitude?

I know that I do not thank you everyday, but I am more than eternally grateful and thankful for the good you've done for me. I am grateful and thankful for all the help I get in life. Just look at it. I needed groceries and my last child paid for some of my groceries. Yes, the bulk of my groceries and now he's doing my laundry for me. Plus, my sister is willing to help pay for my ticket for us to go to Jamaica even though I cannot go to Jamaica. You've forbidden me to go into that dirty land. Yes, I still have things I need to get done. I need that piece of land where I can build our house; home, have a car, plant organic seeds and yes, if permissible; get a good, true, and clean mate.

Yes, we still need our home office for me to write and build you more and more. And yes, bug you more and more. But Lovey, I was thinking about me and a mate and after living so long without one, I don't think I can live with anyone. Not many people can build or comprehend true builders and truth. Yes, the clingy me that live our way Lovey come on now. I truly do not need to live my life for others. As long as we; You and Me Lovey are living right, clean, true, good, ever peaceful good and true, truly happy, ever growing up good and true, and more good and true things, I am more than good to go. I have to think of my life with you Lovey come on now.

I have to be me. I cannot let people influence my truth and true life with you because in true truth, <u>people truly do not know You or Mother Earth Lovey.</u>

God did not make or cause Black Lands to become destitute and unclean. We as Blacks destroyed self, land, our economy, our self worth, and made us destitute and unclean.

We were the ones to believe lies over truth.

We were the ones to accept lies over the truth.

We were the ones to forget the Devil's children and People were the <u>MASTERS OF LIES AND DECEPTION.</u> Thus, billions have and has lost the truth - the True and Living God - Lovey.

Therefore Lovey, I need our bond to be more than solid; impenetrable come on now. I also need this for Mother Earth and us. I need her to be good and true to me and our good and true own Lovey come on now.

You know how I am Lovey come on now. Can Mother Earth not be good and true including truly loyal to our goodness and truth?

Maybe I want and need too much for us Lovey, but I truly don't think so.

Happiness is key for me.

A good and true life is key for me.
Living good and clean is key for me.

Living balanced and harmonious in our environment is key
for me.

Respect of self, others, you Lovey, Mother Earth is key for
me.

Having clean and pure drinking water is key for me.
Having clean and good food is key for me.

Come on Lovey, I have to see clean rivers with the stones at the bottom of the river. You know how I more than loathe any form of dirty water. Yes, I know I can't fight Mother Earth for this; clean and pure drinking water including, rivers and river water, but if I could and win, I would. I don't know but there is something about water that makes me feel whole, pure, great. Water is a true blessing Lovey come on now.

You know me. *MY WATER SHOULD NOT BE SHARED WITH EVIL LANDS COME ON NOW.* No, let me vent with you and to you because I truly can't beat you up for the Waterways of Life.

No, let me hold my temper because despite it all, I know there has to be a better way for the waterways. I refuse to share our water Lovey and you can't make me share. The Waterways of Life, I claim as my own and truly take them from you because to me, you are not doing a very good job of protecting our water, and neither is Mother Earth come on now.

Lovey, do we have to share any water with the different lands?

Yes, I am being a spoilt brat now. But do we have to share any water with the different lands Lovey?

Do you know how precious and sacred water is to me Lovey?

Now tell me Lovey. Is water sacred to You?

Do you have a sacred place here on Earth for me and our good and true people to live where other nations can never ever come in and own land – property?

No Lovey. I am looking at the way some billionaires here on Earth desecrate the sacred land space of others.

White People jus ruin everything. Have no respect for others and their truths – beliefs.

Now Lovey, what about us; the good and true and truly trying to be good here on Earth?

Are you going to let Evil People control us with their ONE WORLD ORDER of cruelty, domination; death?

So, yes Lovey; I am claiming the Waterways as mine. Now tell me, ARE YOU GOING TO GIVE ME MY TRUE DESIRE OF OWNING WATER

THAT IS TRULY AND FULLY INDEPENDENT OF WICKED AND EVIL LANDS?

Yes Lovey, I need you to spoil me more and more in this way.

I need my waterways with you Lovey and Mother Earth as well as, land space with you Lovey and Mother Earth to be fully and truly cut off from other lands, unclean people and beasts, and more.

Truth and true balance Lovey come on now.

Michelle

It's a new day and morning Lovey, May 16, 2021. Truly have a blessed, positive, ever growing good and positive, a truly peaceful day and life, and more good and true goodness. I truly hope you have a blessed, truly peaceful, balanced, harmonious, prosperous, ever growing good day and life continually without end. And yes, I do need all that is good and true for you as I need all that is good and true for me continually without end.

Now Lovey tell me, **WITH ALL THE WHITE RACE HAS AND HAVE DONE TO KILL PEOPLE; HUMANS GLOBALLY, LIE AND DECEIVE NATIONS, AND MORE. DO OR DID THEY NOT THINK THAT YOU WOULD WALK AWAY FROM THEM AND LOCK THEM OUT OF LIFE?**

Just as Babylon did what they did, the White Race did the same. They went against life by lying on life.

Took billions from life.
Killed reckless and rude, and more.

As humans of the different nations:

You cannot go against life and tell lies on the Children and People of Life.

You cannot go against Life – God and tell lies on Life – God and think God will be please with you.

You cannot lie and deceive all and not think God would not be hurt.

You cannot lie and deceive all and not think God would not have a bone to pick with you.

You cannot lie and deceive all and not think God would not lock you out of life.

You cannot lie and deceive all and not think that God would sever all ties with you.

Many Blacks God has and have severed ties with yet, many Blacks truly do not know this.

God gave us everything that is good and true in our land and lands, and we as Black People spat in the Face of God by accepting all that is nasty and unclean.

We as Blacks have and has shamed God. No, don't you dare question this. We did shame God, and we did spit in the Face of God.

Is Religion of God?
Is Religion not of Man?

Did God give anyone here on Earth Religion to curse them and land?

Did God give you the different Gods of Men, and yes; some Women?

Did God give us as Black People or anyone anything nasty – unclean?

God did not give anyone or anything religion to die by.

God did not give humanity death. Humanity gave humanity death.

We as humans created our own death with the sins we do day in and day out. Therefore, it's wise to break away from the lies of the different nations including, the lies of some of our Black Own. And, if you say it about me rest assured you will be punished. You will lose it all.

"TRUTH CANNOT LIE."

Yes, I have faults and God know them trust me on that.

FROM AFRICA TO THE CARIBBEAN AND BEYOND. LOOK AT THE WAY WE AS BLACK PEOPLE SLAUGHTER EACH OTHER WORSE THAN DOGS.

LOOK AT THE WAY MANY HAS AND HAVE BROUGHT EVIL INTO THEIR LAND, AND YOUR LAND TO CONDEMN LAND AND PEOPLE.

Look at Jamaica. God gave Jamaica everything that is blessed and true and look how Jamaicans desecrate the land with obeah, science, death – the killing of each other. <u>NOW THAT GOD HAS AND HAVE WALKED AWAY FROM JAMAICA, FEMALE DEATH OWN THE LAND AND PEOPLE.</u>

No Lovey, instead of keeping true to you and staying true with you, <u>we as Black People slaughter each other for worse than Fools Gold.</u>

We desecrate our Blackness.
Desecrate our Black God.
We desecrate us as a Nation and People.
We desecrate our homes.
We desecrate our life.

We desecrate our values and have become worthless and valueless.

I cannot be this way. Look at how you are showing me things. Again, I am dreaming about Babylon – Babylonian Indians.

Lovey, BABYLON CAN NO LONGER HIDE THE TRUTH OF BLACK PEOPLE.

BABYLON CAN NO LONGER HIDE THE TRUTH OF WHAT THEY DID TO BLACK PEOPLE.

No Lovey, <u>NOTHING MUST STAY HIDDEN FROM BLACK PEOPLE BECAUSE HUNDREDS OF MILLIONS OF BLACKS IF NOT BILLIONS HAVE AND HAS LOST THEIR PLACE WITH YOU DUE TO BELIEF AND CHOICE.</u>

We did accept the different religions of men Lovey come on now. Now tell me, <u>how many in the church will you save?</u>

No, don't be angry with me because; <u>I know none will be saved.</u> <u>WE AS BLACK PEOPLE DID ACCEPT LIES ABOUT YOU.</u>

<u>*WE AS BLACK PEOPLE WERE AND ARE CONDITIONED IN LIES, AND VALUE LIES OVER THE TRUTH.*</u>

Look at the nastiness we accept about you Lovey in the <u>NAME OF RELIGION.</u>

Look at how many Blacks condemn you for the religion and religions they've been conditioned in.

Look how many preachers and teachers spread the lies and deceit including nastiness of the Bible and say, the lies and deceit as well as nastiness of the Bible is of You Lovey.

We both know that the Bible is Death's Book come on now.

When you accept religion and the Bibles of Men:

You have to bow down to Death.

You have to accept Death as your Lord and Personal Saviour.

You have to kill yourself for Death therefore, the Bibles of Men, and Religion.

You have to kill others for Death therefore, the Bibles of Men, and Religion.

You have to turn from Life and turn to Death.

You have to live for Death.

You have to give up Life – the God of Life and Truth – You Lovey.

Look at how we hand down the lies we've been conditioned in to our children and future generations thus locking all/them out of Life – Your Life and World Lovey.

So not tell me Lovey. **HOW CAN WE SAY GOD, WHEN WE TRULY DO NOT KNOW YOU?**

MANY BLACKS DO NOT WANT OR NEED TO HEAR THE TRUTH OF SELF, YOU, OUR TRUE LINEAGE AND LIFE, THE PAST OF BLACKS, AND MORE.

How many Blacks can live with and for truth?

No Lovey. LOOK AT OUR TRACK RECORD WITH YOU.

Now tell me Lovey. WHO HAVE AND HAS LOST OUR TRUTH?

IS IT NOT US AS BLACK PEOPLE?

HAVE WE NOT BECOME THE UNTRUTHFUL AND UNTRUSTWORTHY ONES?

Now Lovey, look at Africa how Africans are so divided that they SLAUGHTER EACH OTHER AND HAVE AND HAS FORGOTTEN THE TRUTH OF LIFE.

Now let me ask you this Lovey. WHY ARE BLACKS CONTINUING TO PLEASE DEATH BY ALLOWING ALL FACETS OF EVIL AND DEATH TO DEVOUR THEM AND THEIR LAND?

No Lovey. LIFE HATH NO MEANING TO BLACK PEOPLE.

LIES ARE THEIR MEANING SO NOW, HOW CAN YOU LOOK TOWARDS THE BLACK

RACE GLOBALLY AND HAVE COMPASSION FOR US?

No, I will not take myself out of this Lovey because at times I cuss you out reckless and rude, I question your integrity, I question you period.

I will not shy away from you Lovey because you are my truth and true source.

No Lovey, look at what we as Black People has and have become globally.

Now tell me Lovey, *WHY DO WE AS BLACK PEOPLE NOT KNOW THAT WHEN WE ACCEPT THE LIES OF OTHERS, WE ARE AND DO FORGET ABOUT YOU, CANNOT KNOW YOU, WE SEVER ALL TIES WITH YOU, CANNOT ATTAIN YOU, CANNOT LIVE WITH YOU, HAVE A DEVIL OF A TIME TO FIND YOU, ARE NOT FORGIVEN IN MANY WAYS FOR OUR WRONGS?*

WE'VE FORGOTTEN THAT:

DISOBEDIENCE IS AUTOMATIC DEATH ONCE THE SPIRIT SHED THE FLESH.

We've forgotten our Blackness Lovey come on now.

We've forgotten you. Can't even find you.

Now tell me Lovey, <u>*HOW MANY AFRICANS*</u>
<u>*WILL SEE YOU AND RESIDE WITH YOU?*</u>

Not all of Africa can be saved because;

<u>AS WHITES HAVE AND HAS
DECEIVED NATIONS, AFRICANS
DID DO THE SAME; DECEIVE THEIR
BLACK OWN.</u>

Yes, we can go back to Africa but Lovey and forgive me here.

<u>WHAT WILL WE AS BLACK PEOPLE
FACE IN AFRICA WHEN WE GO BACK
BLACK? Thus, BLACK TO AFRICA.</u>

<u>I TRUST YOU WITH EVERY FABRIC OF MY
BEING LOVEY THEREFORE, WHEN WE GO
BACK TO AFRICA, WE CANNOT CARRY OUR
CONDITIONED WAY OF THINKING AND
DOING THINGS BLACK, AND BACK WITH US
COME ON NOW.</u>

No Lovey. <u>*I will not have it for our good and true*</u>
<u>*people.*</u> We need to regain life with you therefore,
goodness and truth must truly resonate, live with, and

truly be with us in goodness and truth. I cannot have lands that are filled with evil and strife Lovey come on now. Yes, tongue and teeth will meet, but no bloodshed Lovey come on now.

The way we are living right now is truly not working for us or with us. We can no longer build other nations and not ourselves.

No Lovey. **<u>Look at the riches you've blessed Black Lands and People with and how we've squandered all you've given us in the name of greed.</u>**

Yes Lovey, I have doubts about Black People because I am not having it with them and their short comings and evil. I refuse this for me and you. Therefore, if I am the only one in our land and lands of truth then so be it. I refuse to live ill with anyone therefore, I need good and true peace, good and true harmony, good and true love, good and true growth, good and true planting, good and true happiness, good and true food, good and true health, good and true life. All that is good and true Lovey I more than need in our land and lands with our good and true people. I refuse to plant faulty with you or anyone.

Truth is our stay and word including true love and true growth Lovey come on now.

I need to grow up good and true to you thus, I refuse to be like every Black Person here on Earth and in the Spiritual Realm. I need to be the true and good me with you and to you that I am. My life with you must be continually more than forever ever good and true, truthful, all out more than balanced and harmonious.

I can't give you up even when I want to give you up. Look, I said I needed a vacation from writing and here I am still writing. Therefore, you will not let me give up on you or have any form of vacation from you come on now.

We need to be truly perfect Lovey. With perfection we are truly true, truly giving, truly harmonious, truly peaceful, good and true planters, and more in my view.

Aye Lovey please stay my true one and only because despite my ways, I do truly need and want you. Thus, I seek perfection; all that is good and true from you day in and day out. We have to have our good and true, clean home; house. I crave and yearn this Lovey come on now.

We have to plant good and true not faulty come on now. So yes Lovey, when I look at Africa. I am so disgusted in what Blacks have and has become in the name of greed, forgetting about their Black Roots, Black History, Black Life, You; our Black God Lovey, and more come on now.

Africans are so scattered and divided that I have to wonder if they are TRULY BLACK - ORIGINAL.

Come on Lovey. IF YOU ARE ORIGINAL; WOULD YOU NOT KEEP THE TRUTH, AND CAN SPEAK THE TRUTH OF LIFE.

IF YOU ARE ORIGINAL, WHY ARE AFRICANS NOT TRULY TELLING THE TRUTH OF YOU LOVEY?

IF YOU ARE ORIGINAL, WHY ARE THERE SO MANY TRIBES IN AFRICA?

IF YOU ARE ORIGINAL, WHY ARE YOU SLAUGHTERING EACH OTHER?

IF YOU ARE ORIGINAL, WHY DO SO MANY AFRICANS HAVE MORE THAN ONE WIFE THUS, ACCEPTING THE NASTY AND UNCLEAN WAYS OF BABYLON?

IF YOU ARE ORIGINAL, WHY CAST GOD TO THE SIDE AND ACCEPT DEATH?

WOULD YOU NOT KNOW THE TRUTH OF GOD AND KEPT THE TRUTH AND NOT SEVER ALL TIES WITH GOD; LOVEY?

Yes, Mother Africa asked for prayer. _SHE MOTHER_
AFRICA KNEW WHAT AFRICANS WOULD HAVE,
AND HAS BECOME.

Now tell me Lovey. _DID AFRICANS NOT DOOM_
THEMSELVES TO DEATH?

Mother Africa did turn from you Lovey and she knew
what she did was wrong hence, she did ask me for
prayer long ago. She knew the hell she must face due
to her disobedient own.

Now Lovey. If I was to say seek God, how many will
say; where do I look?

How many will look into themself first?
How many will run to the church?

How many will call their priests, pastor, deacon,
church sister, elder, and more?

How many will sit upright and say God; where do I
look in me to find you and connect with you?

How many will say; God, you and I know I am unclean
and I need to amend my ways. Please help me to find
me and you so that I can be whole and true in you and
with you?

How many will condemn me and these books?

How many will seek Death; their Jesus?

No Lovey, I cannot go out there and minister to people. *These books are our Ministry* – Truth Lovey come on now.

Oh Lord Lovey. I did not get fully into my dreams this morning. Now tell me. *WHAT IS GOING TO HAPPEN IN GUYANA?*

Is happiness going to come Guyana's way? I have to ask Lovey because of my Babylonian dream this morning that had Stacey in the dream.

Is Stacey going to truly find happiness and get married?

Will scamming play a part in her life?

I have to ask Lovey because many of us well not me because I am not in a relationship with anyone apart from you, my guides, all my help in life, and more. But Lovey, what do we do about our Black Men?

So many live for whoredom which is wrong. Now tell me, how do we truly educate our Black Men to respect our Black Women, Self, their Penis, their Life, and stop the whoredom.

This goes for our females too Lovey. How do we truly educate our Black Women and Children to respect Self, their Vagina, their Life, their Penis, their Home, and stop the whoredom?

Whoredom leads to Death Lovey come on now.

When we whore, we Sin and take on the Sins of all we whore with plus come on now.

<u>When are we as humans going to start protecting our life from a life of Sin and Evil – Death?</u>

Oh lord I wish I was at the beach right now soaking up the nice sea breeze and sun enjoying a nice jelly coconut.

Lovey. Black People suh lucky an dem destroy dem luck and truth with you. Man how do I crave the sunshine day in and day out; a place to plant, wash my clothes by the river, bathe in the river, cook by the river, swim in the river. Lovey some have this precious luxury and commodity and destroy it, why?

People nuh noa di preciousness of wata Lovey?

Coo how mi ache and quarrel with you for the Waters of Life.

Yu noa wha. Ole people sey wanti wanti caane getti an getti getti nuh want eee. An Ole People right fi choo.

Lovey, we had you and let you go.

You walked amongst us, an wi lec yu goh; why?

Yu noa wha Lovey.

PEOPLE NUH WANT GOODNESS FI CHOO.

Look how mi plead to yu fi goodness Lovey.
Look how mi plead to yu fi cleanliness.

No Lovey, in our land and lands once all is said and done. I CATEGORICALLY TRULY DO NOT WANT OR NEED ANYONE OR ANYTHING UNCLEAN IN OUR LAND AND LANDS. So, Lovey, do all to keep all undesirables out of our land and lands.

No Lovey. Nuh naasi people or spirit period. I will not have it come on now.

DUTTY CAANE KIP CLEAN.

DUTTY A DUTTY. DUTTY CANNOT BE CLEAN.

And don't go there. No matter how much yu wash yu clothes or home eee still dutty so lang as dutty people inna eee.

No Lovey. Wi balance?
Humans balanced?
Wi thoughts balance; clean all the time?

All wen wi sey wi clean, wi still dutty come on now.

I do not feel to eat and it's after 12pm. I have to get something to eat because I am a bit hungry. Did not have breakfast so now I am going to make something to eat. So, until later Lovey, stay good and true to us and truly help us to make a good and true way for each other, and our good and true own.

Michelle

It's May 17, 2021 and what is going on?

Death was around me this morning.

I dreamt Mother Ford. She was moving from where she lived and moving to Kitchener; the London, Ontario Area. So, I do not know what type of death is going to happen in the Kitchner, London Area.

I dreamt Alton Ellis. In the dream it was Gegory Issacs, but he looked like Alton Ellis. Man did I beat the crap out of him, and threw him out of the house with his fried bacon – meat. He came back in and I draped him up again ready to throw him out. After that I was in this workplace. You know what, let me leave things alone because I know for a fact without doubt Black People will not like me especially the younger generation of Black Females.

Lovey, what is the point in trying to save people – Black People when they truly do not want or need saving?

Are we not trying in vain?

Now Lovey tell me.

If Black People wanted or needed a life of goodness with you, would they not live good and true; clean?

CHEMISTRY by the Reggae Artist Sanchez

It's time to further walk away from Blacks Globally Lovey. Blacks are not saving you.

Blacks did accept all the nastiness of the Devil's Children and People.

Blacks did accept Death as their god.
Blacks are doing all to kill themselves.

No Lovey. It's time you accept the truth. You cannot want good for those who do not want or need good for self.

You cannot save those Blacks who truly do not want or need to be saved.

You cannot continue to lie to yourself when it comes to Blacks. Many cannot be trusted period.

Many cannot be saved because they are in hell already.

Many are loyal to Death hence, the lies we as Blacks tell and hand down from generation unto generation. Therefore Lovey, YOU HAVE TO LEARN TO LIVE WITHOUT BLACKS PERIOD.

No Lovey. Blacks Globally cried for justice yet, are WOLVES IN SHEEP CLOTHING because; when Justice come, we truly do not want it. This is why I tell you to leave the Black Race alone because, I am going to leave them alone to their own demise. Dem too fool fool. They live for Death without knowing this.

You cannot bow down to Death and think it's life; the God of Life – Truth you are bowing down to.

So, however White People continue to use them, rape them of their dignity, wealth, life, self worth, land, You Lovey, and more is truly up to the White Race. I am stepping aside from them; Blacks because; *BLACKS ARE TRULY NOT WORTH IT GLOBALLY.*

I will not take that Black or back Lovey. I am upset this morning because I know the length Black Death will go to wreak havoc on my life in the living.

As for you Lovey, I am upset at you. How can you want us to move back to the Southern Lands of Africa and, not protect the Southern Lands of Africa from Western Investors that will build on peoples sacred land, and destroy the country?

White People have no respect for anything sacred but then, I did dream see White People – this White Man years ago using money as his leverage in Africa therefore, *I will not cry for Black People and their stupidity.*

I will not cry if White People further destroy Black People and Black Lands. I am bleeping fed up of Black People and their stupidity.

F man Lovey. How can we have good and true Black Economy *when the GOVERNMENT AND PEOPLE SELL OUT EVERY DAMNED THING?*

No Lovey. I will not go to the Southern Lands of Africa anymore. You go by yourself because I am mad this morning.

No Lovey not with this. How the hell can you say and not protect the Southern Lands of Africa. You were not true then come on now.

How the hell can we have our own when you have not honestly and truly provided for us; our good and true own and truly trying?

How can you Lovey and Mother Earth continue to let the Super Rich – freaking White Billionaires get away with murder; what they are doing globally?

You Lovey and Mother Earth truly do not care. This is not dungeons and dragons come on now. Yes, people need jobs but, *IT IS US AS BLACK PEOPLE THAT SHOULD BE BENEFITING FROM BLACK LANDS, AND WEALTH COME ON NOW.*

I HAD SO MUCH HOPE FOR US IN THE SOUTHERN LANDS OF AFRICA AND NOW YOU'VE RAPED ME OF MY DREAM LOVEY. HOW COULD YOU?

The planting.

The homes we would build to help those who are in need in the Southern Lands of Africa.

The giving of goodness and truth that I needed us to do Lovey is all gone now because you took my right and truth from me.

No, you are truly not fair in this way. You keep robbing me of my truth, true right, true justice, true giving, truth of life; why?

Why do you continually disappoint me in this way?

Now tell me, who is benefitting from all this?

It's truly not the land and people.

No Lovey, I should have known that you would turn around and disappoint me. I was too happy, and you cannot stand seeing me happy day in and day out.

No Lovey, you are being unfair and unjust. I need happiness each and every day, but you had to throw a wrench into the plans I need with you.

No Lovey, *THE HOGS THAT RUN BLACK LANDS F THEM ALL.*

Life comes down to the dollar bill for them.
Life comes down to destroying Black Lands for them.

Life comes down to raping their land and people of its wealth and their wealth.

I will not blast you this morning Lovey because I should have known just how stupid and greedy some Blacks are therefore, their land and people are valueless to them. Money and greed is key to their life period.

So yes, Blacks will truly hate me but F all who hate me.

NO WEAPON – *Fred Hammond*

So, no matter how they send the dead for me, feed the dead for me in hopes that the dead will kill me, goh a obeah man and oman for me, will do all to conquer and kill me they will categorically fail.

No Lovey, a suh Black People....no, don't ask that question Michelle. If Blacks cannot defend their own Black God, they will not defend you, they will do all to devour and kill you.

Lovey when did Black People become so demonic?

No, that was a stupid question Lovey. *JUST AS YOU HAVE WHITE DEMONS YOU HAVE BLACK DEMONS ALSO.* Those Blacks that say they are with you but behind your back, they do all to crucify you, sell you out, and do all to kill you.

So no, Black People don't want goodness for self. Goodness is an illusion for them. But how could you Lovey *SELL ME OUT JUST LIKE THAT WHEN IT COMES TO THE SOUTHERN LANDS OF AFRICA?*

I trust you Lovey, but how can you break me and break my trust just like that man?

I don't know but I am disappointed in you this morning thus, I am writing of my disappointment.

Why show me the Southern Lands of Africa lined in gold to now disappoint me like this?

Now tell me Lovey and truly forgive me for this. But Lovey, *ARE YOU MY WEAPON IN LIFE?*

Meaning, are you like unto those ungrateful and lying Blacks that say they are with you and behind your back they are doing all to set you up, destroy and kill you, and more?

Trust and true trust Lovey. So now tell me, why are you breaching my trust in you?

Why do you want and need me to doubt and cuss you out this morning?

Have you changed your mind about the Southern Lands of Africa?

This morning Lovey. Have you become my enemy?

No Lovey, have you become my enemy this morning?

Lovey, listen to me. Dirty is truly not clean.

You cannot want a place for us, and not clean it properly for us and our good and true own only.

Why give dirty?

If a land and place is truly not clean, why want us to go there?

Are we not dirtying self and you when we go into dirty lands?

Are you not calling down death and destruction upon us Lovey?

Yes, I know you are God, but why give faulty and unclean?

You do not give you faulty and unclean then, don't do it to me and our people come on now.

Why do I bother Lovey?
Why do I bother?

You can't even give me breakfast in bed.

I don't know Lovey. I want to cry but I will not cry. I have to hold on to hope that you know best, and you will let everything work out good and true for our good and true own.

Right now, I am at a loss Lovey. I so wanted to develop and plant truly perfect; good and true with you.

Why take away my gain and hope with you Lovey?

Why do you continually build greedy and unclean people?

No Lovey. Justice – True Justice is not unclean.

True Justice is Just come on now.

So now tell me, why can't you live fair and just with me?

Why take my salvation with you from me?

Why disappoint me?
Why ruin me and my hope?

Why leave me hopeless and confused on some days?

No Lovey man. Stand up and stand with me for that which is truly right and just.

Hold my hand truthfully and build with me good and clean; truly true and good, ever growing good and true, positive, just, balanced, harmonious, and more good and true things.

No Lovey. Instead of building us continually without doubt and fault, you allow doubt and fault to come in on some days and I am truly sick of this doubt and fault when it comes to me and you.

You know what, *YOU LOVE TO SEE WHEN I ARGUE WITH YOU.* No, that's it. You truly love to see when I argue with you and cuss you out on some days. But Lovey, yu nuh come back with flowers of the most beautiful kind, kiss me on the cheek, and say you are sorry for getting me upset.

So yes, yu faulty Lovey. No, don't be angry. The Flowers and apology. And that's all I am going to say.

Michelle

Aye Lovey, you have a way of letting me find things and shake me up.

Yes, no matter how much good you want and do for your people, it will never be good enough for some. At the end of the day, they taint your image and do all matter of evil to harm and discredit you. Thus, humans globally has and have done this to you. See, all facets of religion and religious beliefs, our sins, our way of living, our unjust law and laws, and more.

No, I will not get into the issues Shaggy is having with the Bustamante Children's Hospital in Jamaica because, it is truly not my concern. *Shaggy, if the hospital is due their 100 million dollars, give it to them truthfully and in goodness and truth.* You are wrong to hold on to the money. You are committed to pay the hospital $100 million dollars you collected for them via your charity fund raising. It was and is wrong for you to hold on to monies owing to them.

Any interest collected belong to the Hospital because, you are holding on to money owing to them. Yes, in truth, the Interest belong to your Foundation. You did collect it on the behalf of the hospital. However, the interest belongs to the hospital. *You can come to an agreement for the interest with the hospital and use the interest to build 2 or 3 homes for those who are truly in need in Jamaica.* There are families out there that are living in unfavourable situations. Help them too. *Once things have and has been resolved* _with Bustamante Children's Hospital sever ties with the Hospital._

I will not give you right when you are truly wrong.

For the future, _TAKE YOUR GOODNESS OUT OF JAMAICA._ Think Africa and doing something and or, help the poor and needy on that continent or another Caribbean Island. _DO FOR PEOPLE WHO ARE THANKFUL AND GRATEFUL. But, you are categorically wrong for holding on to funds raised for Bustamante Children's Hospital._

OR

Uses your resources to help schools in Jamaica that need funding.

Like I said, build homes for the poor and needy.

There are people in Jamaica that has medical issues, help garner help to help those people that need to go oversees for medical aide.

Yes, I know I said, your issue is not my concern and I've put my two cents in. _BUT AS A JAMAICAN, YOU OF YOURSELF SHOULD KNOW THAT NO MATTER HOW YOU TRY TO HELP YOUR_

OWN, YOUR OWN WILL DO ALL TO TAKE YOU DOWN AND TARNISH YOUR IMAGE.

Remember:

MARCUS MOSIAH GARVEY and how he was set up by his own for the good he was doing to educate and help his Black Own.

PAUL BOGLE and how he died trying to help his Black Own.

ROBERT NESTA MARLEY AND PETER TOSH and how they in Jamaica did all to kill the both of them.

More importantly, remember *GOD* and how God has and have tried to help us as Black People, and daily we continue to spit in the face of God with our lies and deceit.

GOODNESS DO COME AT A COST IT SEEMS AND IT SHOULD NOT BE THIS WAY BUT IT IS. *Meaning, goodness do come at a cost if you are helping the wicked and evil.*

Further,

GOODNESS DO COME AT A COST "IF YOU ARE NOT CLEAN OR HAVE GOOD AND CLEAN; TRUE INTENTIONS."

So, if you owe the hospital their money; give it to them and end this bickering.

You raised this money to help the hospital then let there be no waiting for the funds. I am tired of hearing it. *THERE SHOULD BE NO BICKERING OVER MONEY RAISED TRUTHFULLY FOR A GOOD AND TRUE CAUSE COME ON NOW MAN.*

Your name should not be dragged through the mud for the good you are trying to do. Think of your family and your reputation.

You have a foundation. Your foundation should not be faulty, nor should thievery be associated with your efforts. What you are telling people when you do not turn funds over to the hospital is that; *YOU ARE NO BETTER THAN THE JAMAICIAN POLITICIANS OF HOGS THAT ROB THEIR PEOPLE AND LAND BLIND OF THEIR SELF WORTH AND DIGNITY.*

WHEN YOU WITHHOLD THE MONEY OWING TO THE BUSTAMANTE CHILDREN'S HOSPITAL, YOU ARE SAYING YOU ARE A LIAR AND A THIEF.

You cannot have a foundation that raises money to help others and not do what you are supposed to do.

You are telling me and the world that; *YOU ARE A SCAMMER AND YOU CANNOT BE TRUSTED* when you withhold funding from the source and people you are trying to help.

Yes, you can tell me to shut the F up because I truly do not know the situation or you. I am interfering where I should not. However, *LOOK INTO YOU AND WHAT YOU SHAGGY AND YOUR FOUNDATION STAND FOR.*

If you have no ethics, then have no foundation. Truly do not help because *YOU ARE ADDING SIN TO YOUR SIN RECORD AND PLATE AND TRUST ME, HELL IS TRULY NOT PRETTY.*

Yes, I see your plight and God is just teaching me of the way some of us as Blacks are. Like Bugle sey; you can do 99 good and the 1 good you cannot do to make a hundred, people drag you through the mud and slander you. So yes, *God is cautioning me on my goodness.* It's good to want, but it's not many that can appreciate true goodness therefore, *IT IS WISE AND TRUE TO KNOW WHO YOU EXTEND AND GIVE GOODNESS TO.* Thus, I will still say you are wrong to withhold funds to Bustamante Children's Hospital.

You cannot keep what truly do not belong to you. If you cannot give all the money at once, make true and good arrangements to give what you have and let things go. *And no, di craven hog dem inna government out there should not charge you taxes on GOODNESS.*

So yes, *GOD IS GOOD* because; despite my anger, *God do find a way to show me things when it comes to giving by the afternoon or evening* as it is 1:45 pm Monday afternoon.

So yes, truly thank you Lovey because I would never ever have a Foundation in your honour. I more than truly loathe Foundations.

FOUNDATIONS ARE SCAMS.

Therefore, Foundations rob people of their truth and wealth whist fattening the pockets of those who run the different Foundations globally.

So, for all who think they are being blessed when they give to the different foundations, you are truly not blessed. You are foolishly giving away your blessing.

If you have it to give. It is better to build a home or two for the needy in the land you desire; truly love, and let your blessings flow that way.

When you go on vacation carry a backpack if you can afford one and give it to a child in need. Tell God what you need to do good and true before hand, and let God open a clean, safe, and true way for you to give so that your blessing can flow.

Michelle

BOOKS WRITTEN BY MICHELLE JEAN 2021

MY TALK JANUARY 2021

MY TALK JANUARY 2021 – BOOK TWO

MINI BOOK

JUST TALKING – THINKING

A LITTLE TALK WITH MOTHER EARTH

I NEED ANSWERS GOD

POETRY MY WAY

THE MIND AND SPIRITUALITY

I NEED ANSWERS GOD – PART TWO

MY NIGHTS

I NEED ANSWERS GOD – PART THREE

COMING SOON

WHAT ABOUT US